The Petite Kitchen

*A short book
by a short girl
about the healing magic of her kitchen*

Written by
Francine Campanelli

"A recipe has no soul.
You, as the cook,
must bring the soul to the recipe."

Thomas Keller

*If you have ever shared a seat around my table,
this memoire is dedicated to you.*

*And to a wonderful being who held my hand
as we walked each other home.*

The Table

Before my father passed away he brought one of my dreams to life. He helped and taught my son how to build a sturdy rustic table. A table large enough to sit ten people. A table strong enough to hold many trays without wobbling. A table that would be the center of my kitchen and home. And she came to be.

This table has heard the celebratory clinking of glasses, has been witness to many a grieving heart and has healed so many souls who have sat around her. With a coat of white paint I dry brushed onto her and a distressed finish, she does not mind when red wine spills, when sparklers have fallen on her and created tiny burns on her strong top or when bubbling roasts are placed on her for everyone to enjoy. She is the foundation to my healing kitchen. She is who holds the teacups of magic and infused water and meals I present to those I love or in need of nourishment. She's memorized my children's laughter and soothed their worries. It is her I leaned onto in disbelief when I heard of my father's passing and when I received my divorce paperwork unexpectedly. And it is also her I've held onto laughing, leaning over to blow out birthday candles and serving wine to the man I love sitting across from me as we celebrate Un-Valentines.

She is a hopeless romantic, a nurse, a shaman, a healer, a therapist. She is my table.

I hear a knock at my door. I answer and there stands my friend trying to find solace from the heat that has been plaguing us. I let her in and offer her a seat at the table. I place a cold glass bottle of infused water for her to drink. Her baby is fussy. She just got out of work and an angry summer sun has been beating on us as if we were paying penance for sins we have yet to commit.

Her eyes look sunken, her skin tired. I pour some of the magic elixir into a glass goblet full of ice. The summery yet refreshing scent of rosemary, mint and lemon zest fill the room as her goblet is filled.

Rosemary is soothing, it's a destressing and cooling herb. We both need it. Rosemary is also helpful with allergies which are prominent during this season. Mint is refreshing, she helps to relax yet wakes you up just as lemon does. I see my friend take a deep breath and close her eyes. I can tell all she needed was to sit down and hydrate herself.

The elixir of delicately infused water flows freely. Her baby falls asleep as we talk quietly. I place a fresh salad in front of her. A simple plate full of arugula and spinach tossed with feta cheese and pickled beets dressed gracefully in a light drizzle of olive oil, balsamic vinegar, freshly ground pepper and pink salt. Uncomplicated yet nourishing. No need for the euphoria induced by a glass of iced coffee served in a plastic cup, no need for processed meats lazily tossed between bread. Nothing but fresh, living, gorgeous gifts from the garden today. She smiles.

Infused Water Elixir
Glass pitcher or bottle
Alkaline or Spring Water
Sprigs of Rosemary
Sprigs of Mint
A couple peels of lemon rind
Combine
Be creative and follow your instinct, if your intuition calls for a certain herb use it.
Cool.
Enjoy.

Teacups

  I can't stop coughing. I've been trying to steer clear of my family as much as I can as to not get them sick. The wind outside my window is howling. Such a temperamental being. I pray under my breath it's not related to the virus that has been going around and thankfully it isn't.
  My body calls for something warm and soothing. For whatever reason by throat can't tolerate fire cider at the moment as it aggravates my cough. I truly believe fire cider is great as a preventative and I know I should have started taking it when the weather changed its mask.

I wrap my sweater tightly around me and go outside to clip a few sprigs in my herb garden. Oregano is a must, she's a magical all-natural antibiotic and expectorant. I dug out a piece of ginger. It's a miracle this warming rhizome is still going. And I am grateful it is as it is a wonderful and tasty expectorant.

I put a small glass pot with water to boil once I'm back to the warmth and safety of my kitchen. I can hear the wind whistle a tune to which the frogs reply with a sharp melancholy I find soothing this evening. I cut a few round slices of ginger and add them to the pot. In go a few sticks of fragrant cinnamon and the sprigs of oregano. I let it boil for five minutes then cover my pot, turn off the flame, and let this healing concoction steep for another five.

I grab my colander and I can see my chickens outside my window playing in the wind. Instead of them seeking the warm comfort of their coop they are chasing a small squirrel that snuck into their area in hopes of filling his cheeks with grain and seeds.

As my tea steeps, I go to my China cabinet. My dear thrift store find with its French provincial details and coats of white paint I bathed it in. Inside of its doors, its belly, different porcelain teacups sleep. Pastel hand painted roses or tiny swirls adorn each one. Each one with its own personality. I choose a pastel beauty as graceful and light as air.

Each teacup holds a different story. Gifts, thrift store finds, estate sales. Yet they all hold the same daintiness bone China is famous for. And all of them are adorned in soft delicate pastels. They always manage to make me smile.

I pour the tea through a colander into a white teapot and sit at my table. Some honey and a slice of lemon go into my cup. The aromatic hot tea makes the honey disappear and the lemon's citrusy aroma carries itself gently in the steam. I take a tiny sip. A deep breath. I know I'll feel better by the morning.

My Firey Cider

32 oz Glass jar with non metallic lid
2-4 serrano peppers, split
Handful of fresh Rosemary sprigs
Handful of fresh Oregano sprigs
Handful of fresh Thyme sprigs
Peeled cloves from 1 head of garlic
2 lemons, sliced
1 red onion quartered
1 cup raw honey
Organic apple cider vinegar
Put all ingredients into the jar.
Top off with the apple cider vinegar.
Cover tightly and store in your fridge for at least two weeks.
Once it is ready, take 1-2 tablespoons a day during cold season as a preventative.

The Chair

There he stands. The handsome rickety thing. With a loose rung and chippy paint yet standing strong. Like a knight who returned from a battle. Who knows how long he has been around, how many have sat and rested on him. The conversations he must have heard. He sits quietly and watches me cook for my family on a daily basis.

That's my preferred chair. This is where I sit before the house stirs awake. I prepare my tea or my coffee and sit enveloped in the stillness and quiet of the kitchen. Sometimes I play some Chet Baker or Blossom Dearie to break the silence and dance in my chair.

Today it's breakfast for one. The children are away on their travels. I have my usual- jasmine matcha tea, raw honey, slice of lemon. The hens have laid their beautiful greenish blue eggs. Nothing is better than a farm fresh egg. I know I'll be having one for breakfast today.

Scrambled eggs with vegetables sound perfect this morning. No need for bread. Nothing too heavy but yet filling enough to get my day started well. I turn around and see that I have a lot of tomatoes and serrano peppers I harvested. Before they go spend the rest of their days in the compost bin I decide to make a simple salsa. That will be a great addition to my veggie scramble.

I place 5 tomatoes in a pot of water as well as 2 serrano peppers and bring them to a boil. When I see the skin on the tomatoes start to crack and peel I turn off the flame and remove the tomatoes and peppers. I place them in my blender along with 4 peeled cloves of garlic and some salt to taste. I puree them and my salsa is ready. This is a wonderful base for a chunkier "dipping salsa". Just add diced onion and cilantro and there you have it. Simple yet with a bite.

I prepare my vegetables and cook them accordingly, scrambling into them the tasty eggs. Once they are ready I pull out a chair, my favorite chair, and sit down. I take a sip of my tea and give my thanks to the universe for the beautiful nourishing food that sits in front of me. I feel spoiled.

Vegetable and Egg Scramble

2 tablespoons unsalted butter
1 tablespoon mild oil of your choice
1 small golden potato, diced
½ medium zucchini, diced
1 small tomato, diced
¼ red onion, chopped
1 handful fresh spinach
2 eggs
¼ cup grated parmigiano
¼ cup heavy cream
Garlic salt and freshly ground pepper

Melt butter in pan, add oil and potatoes.
Cook under medium low flame until potatoes are golden and cooked through.
Add the rest of the vegetables and sauté until onions become semi translucent.
In a bowl, scramble your eggs with the parmigiano and cream adding garlic salt and pepper to taste.
Add the eggs to your pan and scramble.
When eggs are almost cooked through add spinach and continue scrambling.
Serve with toasted buttered sourdough.
Share.

The Platter

I remember the day I found him. He stood out amongst the brick a brack and mismatched dinnerware at the thrift store. I collect vintage platters and tureens and finding him on that shelf in all his crazed and faded glory was unexpected. It was a miracle he was complete and all edges intact. No chips whatsoever. I don't remember what I paid for this beautiful piece of China but I know it was not much as this was before the reselling phenomena took over. How I miss those days!

Platters this size are great for serving one of my favorite dishes, pasta! Pasta al limone to be exact. This is such a delicious and light yet creamy pasta that's extremely simple and quick to make.

Whenever I get a porcelain or ceramic dish that has been preloved and discarded, I make sure to clean it gently yet well. If there are cracks, I use them for display only but if there is only a bit of crazing and its whole I breathe life into it in my kitchen.

Any stains are easily removed gently and efficiently using a squirt of lemon and peroxide mixed with baking soda and turned into a paste. I spread this evenly on area I am treating and leave it on for a couple of hours. It also works great as a degreaser on delicate pieces too.

I scrub the paste off using a microfiber cloth or a no scratch scrubbing pad. If the stain remains, retreat the area. And if it doesn't go away at all, let it be. It's the imperfections that make older pieces perfect.

After cleaning and drying my imperfectly perfect old yet new to me platter I proceeded to cook my pasta. And it was a great choice as this is a quick pasta to make and its super easy too!

I cook one pound of bucatini until it is al dente according to the package directions. Once cooked I drain it and reserve ½ cup of the pasta water and return the bucatini to the pot. I stir in ½ cup of unsalted butter, a small drizzle of extra virgin olive oil and stir rapidly. To this I add ½ a cup of finely grated parmigiano and ¼ cup pecorino. Continue stirring quickly and add pasta water little by little if your pasta looks too dry. It should look moist but not soggy or saucy. Squeeze a whole lemon into your pasta and throw it in, peels and all and continue rapidly stirring. Add salt and pepper to taste and serve.

As delicious as pasta is, pasta can be quite heavy specially if eaten at later hours. For this we need a digestif. In the form of tea of course! I fill my kettle with fresh water and let it sit patiently over a flame until it is hot enough to awaken the healing properties of the wonderful plants he is about to bathe. I sit and wait.

Liquid Digestif
2 Cups fresh spring or alkaline water
1 Teaspoon fennel seeds
2 Teabags chamomile
1 Teaspoon dried orange peel
1 Mint teabag or 1 tablespoon fresh mint
Bring water to a boil.
Place the rest of ingredients in a mesh teabag and into a teapot.
Pour boiling water into the teapot and let it steep five minutes.
Remove mesh teabag.
Serve.
Pinky's up.

The Spoon

She could be a collector's item the way she shines, and her intricate pattern unfolds throughout her handle. How can something made of solid silver be so dainty and graceful? Maybe she is a collector's item but when I chose her and her brothers from a pile of flatware and cutlery I did it for her looks, and the story she might have hidden in the tarnish that dotted her like a stubborn beauty mark. My spoon.

My silver spoon that filled my son's fat cheeks full of pureed vegetables, that stirred my father's coffee in the evening. The spoon I use to sneak a bite of crème fraiche from the refrigerator. The spoon that will outlive me.

My neighbor visits. She wants to find love. Solace makes her heart ache she says. She wishes for a companion, for some sweetness in her life. I put before her a small china bowl filled with shortbread cookies. Shortbread cookies are glamorous to me. Like a little black dress. They go well with anything- from tea, lemonade to a strong espresso. Weddings, births, birthdays and even funerals- they are always appropriate and welcomed. She takes a bite, smiles and asks me for the recipe.

The recipe is simple. A half cup of European style unsalted butter is crumbled into ¼ cup of white sugar, 1 teaspoon pure vanilla extract and 1 cup of flour. You mix this by hand and press the dough into a small ceramic tray where I slice the dough with a knife. Each cookie should be about ¼ inch thick. I bake them in a preheated 350-degree oven for 15-20 minutes. It's that simple.
    She nods and smiles again. There is a second of silence and she looks up. She asks about my garden; I tell her the tomatoes did not survive the heatwave and my lettuce bolted early. We talk about what we will be sharing with our loved ones in the upcoming holidays and whether we will be staying in town or traveling. She'll be traveling and I'll be staying. She continues telling me how lonely winter is, especially around the holidays. I ask her if she can have anything she wishes for what would it be. Without hesitation she responds, "Love."
    I place a teacup and my spoon in front of her and tell her to make a wish.

Wishing Spell

To attain-

Stir tea or coffee in a clockwise motion concentrating on what it is you want that you know will positively impact and benefit you without harming others.

To banish-

Stir tea or coffee in a counter-clockwise motion concentrating on what it is you need to rid of in your life that is halting your growth or bringing negativity into your world.

The Glass Jar

    One holds müesli, one holds baking soda, one is pregnant with rum soaked raisins, another one is barely filled with the brown sugar I make. I need to make some more to fill this jar with. I grab the glass jar of sticky dark molasses from my pantry as well as the cane sugar. I pour some of the glittery sugar into a bowl and slowly add and stir the molasses into it, just enough to color my sugar and turn it from beige to a beautiful brown.

    With my old patinaed wooden spoon I scoop my homemade brown sugar into the glass jar and tightly seal it. One less thing to worry about.

Worry. I hate how this word has become a part of many of our vocabularies the last couple of years. Finances, epidemics, politics, children's safety at school… Not only do we have the normal daily "just because I'm living" things to worry about but add that list to the mix and it's not a pretty feeling.

I'm grateful nature is our ally. I feel blessed to have an herb garden. I am thankful to the bee farmers and the raw honey they provide for us. I grab my basket and shears and head outside, just the breeze hitting my face seems to soothe my worries away.

Anti Anxiety Oxymel

Glass Jar
Organic (preferable raw) apple cider vinegar
Raw Honey
Equal parts roughly chopped fresh chamomile flower, lemon balm and fresh organic lavender blooms- enough to fill up your jar.
Pour enough honey to cover ¾ of your jar.
Fill the remainder of your jar with honey leaving a ½ inch headspace.
Cover and give it a good shake.
Let sit in a dark pantry for 4-6 weeks, will keep for 2 years.
Enjoy a teaspoon or two daily with your tea or add to dressings.
Relax.

The Vase

White roses, eucalyptus fronds, purple splashes of Limonium. I bring the flowers to my nose and breathe it all in. I wish I could bottle the feeling, the smell forever. My heart smiles and my face shows it. He has no idea how happy this gesture has made me.

I grab a stepping stool and reach for a milk glass vase in my kitchen cabinet. I cradle her gently in my hands, this beautiful flea market find. She is shaped like a woman's hand holding a vase. Stark white, heavy yet fragile and unique. Another old treasure that is precious to me.

I cut of the ends of the bouquet and gently place the flowers into the cool water I poured into my vase. Lovely. I stand back to admire my roses. It should be a rule that puppies and bouquets live forever.

We eat dinner and talk about our day. I can't help but to take loving glances here and there at my flowers sitting elegantly in their vase. Nature for the win. I am in love.

My last bite is of my favorite side dish, candied yams. It's so simple yet so amazing. I peel, boil, drain and mash a couple of sweet potatoes. I add plenty of unsalted butter and a splash of heavy cream to them. I stir in brown sugar, just enough to make it pleasantly sweet, a pinch of salt, a splash of vanilla extract and a few dashes of pumpkin spice and cinnamon before topping it off with mini marshmallows and placing this dish in the oven until it heats through. Leftovers are amazing with a cold glass of milk! But I will wait until tomorrow for that.

Tonight, however, there will be no milk but champagne with a hibiscus bloom in syrup to celebrate love and friendship. The beautiful sound of the cork popping startles me and I laugh. Bubbles pour freely throughout the night. A boozy night filled with great conversation, music, laughter and flirtatious touches here and there.

I think this is what I love to refer to as a perfect evening!

Hibiscus Blooms in Syrup

½ Cup hibiscus (Jamaica) dried blooms
1 Cup spring water
½ cup sugar
Bring water to a boil.
Add hibiscus blooms and lower the flame.
Let blooms steep for 3 minutes and with a slotted spoon remove them and set them aside in a glass jar.
Add sugar to your water and stir until it fully dissolves.
Pour your syrup over your hibiscus blooms and let cool.
Serve syrup and a bloom in a champagne flute and pour the bubbly of your choice over it.
Cheers!

The Mug

 She didn't fit in. Her color was different than the rest. But he loved her and God forbid it would fall and shatter or I'd get rid of her. It was his favorite mug.

 Every morning I would hear my father's heavy steps as he slowly went down the stairs to make himself his morning coffee. And evening too. Strong, overly sweet and of course poured in his favorite mug. That bright odd mug with a red blossom tattooed obnoxiously on its porcelain skin. For years since my parents divorced, he carried her with him like a reminder of a life past.

She stuck out like a sore thumb amongst the pastel and alabaster white mugs that sat beside her in the cabinet. He'd brew a strong pot of coffee and sometimes he would let me sweeten it for him with a lazy pour of condensed milk. The result was a thick, rich and creamy caffeine kick. But he preferred 2 heaping tablespoons of sugar, no cream. I always found this too sweet but maybe it was his way of sweetening all the bitterness he had lived through as a child and young man.

However, on cold nights my father preferred his "Lung Warming Tea." He claimed it would warm you up from the inside out and make you sweat any symptoms of a cold or cough you may be harboring. I have to say I have proven this to be true and have stopped a cold in it's tracks with this tea many times. The smell of cinnamon, liquor and honey would hug us during the evenings he would drink his tea and to this day, when the smell of cinnamon and brandy fill the air I can almost feel my dad hug me and say, "It's a good night for tea."

Lung Warming Tea

Stainless steel or glass pot
2 cups alkaline or spring water
3 cinnamon sticks
1 shot glass of brandy (please omit if it is to be shared to those who are not of age to consume alcohol)
1 tbsp raw honey

Pour water into your pot and add your cinnamon sticks.
Bring to a slow boil then remove from heat and cover letting it steep for approximately 5 minutes. Pour into your mug along with the shot of brandy. Sweeten with honey and feel the spicy, boozy goodness hug you from the inside out.

The Napkins

A stack of stained cotton squares sits before me. Although they just came out of the wash, they look dingy and forlorn. Years of sitting on laps catching gravies, syrups, buttery fingers and vinaigrettes. They have been kissed by hundreds of lips and wiped up many a spill. These ancient cotton table napkins have been witnesses to so many dinner parties they maybe should be disposed of, but I don't think they should retire yet.

It's the first day of a new month and all bills have been paid. Business has been slow and there is no need to be wasteful. Giving objects in my home a new life is a priority to me and is a good way to save money. Also, it's the perfect day to perform a money spell. But first. I'll be dying my cloth napkins naturally and frugally.

I place a liter of water to boil into a large pot and place her over the flame. I throw in one quarter of a cup of salt, 20 bags of black tea and a half cup of white vinegar as it boils. I stir it well. I add all the cotton napkins into the tea concoction and stir them around making sure they all drink up the vinegary tea "broth" which will act like a natural dye. I let my napkins boil for twenty minutes and then leave them overnight soaking up the beautiful earthy color the tea has shared with them.

I wake up early to feed my hens and hurry to get back indoors to rinse and wash the napkins I left soaking the night before. A good rinse with cold water and soap flakes then off to set in the dryer they go!

I place them in the highest setting in the dryer and when the cycle is finally done, I take them out, fold them and press them with my hand into tidy squares. The stains have hidden within the earthy brown color of my napkins now and they are ready for their new life as breadbasket and harvest basket liners. I am so glad they still have a use in my home.

Money Spell

Ground cinnamon

Your front door

On the first of the month open the front door to your home and stand outside of it looking in. Sprinkle a good amount of ground cinnamon onto the palm of your right hand (this is your receiving hand) and concentrate on the abundance you are ready to receive.

Open yourself to receiving financial abundance and success as you blow the cinnamon into your home. Smile and walk back into your home closing the door behind you.

Have faith that nothing but positive financial situations will come to you and any expense will be readily covered.

Goodnight

One by one candles are blown out. Some lights are turned off while others are simply dimmed as to scare away any monsters hiding in the nooks of my kitchen. China rests alongside spoons. There are forks and ladles drying sleepily upon tea towels. The scent of cinnamon and the faint nuance of vanilla permeate the air. I breathe it all in as I untie my apron and hang it on the pantry door where it will be waiting for me till the next sunrise and accompany me while I sink my fingers in dough, crack an egg, stir my tea and welcome the day in this part of my home where love, gastronomic alchemy and the smell of spices and fresh herbs await. It can only happen in one place……

The Petite Kitchen

Made in the USA
Middletown, DE
26 March 2023